I0192566

WRITING RUMI

POEMS ALONG AN ILLUMINATED WAY

WRITING RUMI

POEMS ALONG
AN ILLUMINATED WAY

BARBARA BUCKNER

EPIGRAPH BOOKS
RHINEBECK, NEW YORK

Writing Rumi: Poems Along an Illuminated Way © 2020 by Barbara Buckner

All rights reserved. No part of this book may be used or re-produced in any manner without the consent of the author except in critical articles or reviews. Contact the publisher for information.

The writings in this book reflect the author's own spiritual understanding and are not intended to speak for any spiritual path, teacher, or religion. In rare instances, the author uses certain terms trademarked by Eckankar and intends fair use of these terms, whose trademark usage rights belong solely to Eckankar.

Paperback ISBN 978-1-951937-48-5
eBook ISBN 978-1-951937-49-2

Library of Congress Control Number 2020911703

Book design by Colin Rolfe

Epigraph Books
22 East Market Street, Suite 304
Rhinebeck, NY 12572
(845) 876-4861
epigraphps.com

Dedicated to Divine Love, the Source of All

Looking

Cat calls and juniper trails,
Where will I not go looking for You?
Even if friends betray me and roads disappear in the brush,
What will I not use to seek You?
Please play a symphony from a tree
Or leave a sign on a tree stump.
My ears can hear whispers one thousand miles from here,
Like lampposts dispelling street darkness
    in an other-world neighborhood.
Let me find You – or be found –
I am lost, and Love is all around me.

Wherever I Go

Wherever I go, there you are.
You hold me as tenderly as a nest does a robin's egg
Or light that caresses freshly fallen snow on a trail.
If a bird takes wing, you are the wind that helps it fly,
And when snow melts in spring, you are the lake
    it disappears in.
If I forget you, you hunt me down with pricks of loneliness,
And if I lose sight of you, you put up a mirror to reflect
    what I am missing.
If I'm listless, you take my hand and turn the page,
And if I sleep too long, the lamp of your eyes awakens me.
If I go to the desert, you live in the tent I have yet to erect,
If I go back to the city, you've arranged for my family
    to greet me.
When I ask the difficult question your silence speaks
    louder than my voice,
And when I hear thunder on the mountaintop,
It's the step I take as your disciple.

Blue Cup

The ocean breaks open in electric blue –
My hands cup its deep roar,
Blue for royal, and white for logic.

Waves are like hair on the strand,
Stars are like white teeth in the grass.
My body's immersed in a cup of blue wind,
Salting the flavor of this sacred skin.

Hidden

Like a wick hidden in candle flame
Or soldiers camouflaged in green thicket,
My joy is hidden in the wings of your theater,
Whose actors are Light and Sound, earth and water,
And the lines are all laughter authored by the poet of life –
Awesome Trouble!

Finally

For Moses, the Red Sea parted,
For me, the fruitless dance stopped.
No longer hearing madmen's music
I began to witness marvels –
Not in succession like pompous kings,
But singularly and deliriously, like joy.

Dance where you are – it being the best of places –
The diamond cutter will bring you the ring of life
Studded with jewels, and finally Grace.

Nearer

We are closer than air, we two,
Closer than flower and stamen, rock against earth.
Enlist me in your dream of nearness,
Nearer to me I am – you being me,
Exalted.

In These

In solitude, contentment.
In stillness, the moment.
In age, endurance.
In strength, the future.
In Sound, the source.

Watching

A wounded horse fell on the trail,
I loved its shiny golden tail.

A drunk stumbled in the gutter,
I loved the truth of God she uttered.

A blizzard felled a mangy cat,
I loved his regal face like that.

A couple died in freezing rain,
I watched two Souls rise up again.

You take from me all things at last,
And give me Freedom,
    the breath that lasts.

Code

Your mouth opens simply,
No letters are necessary.
In a dream where vowels are messages
And talk is a dance between flaming heads,
I am sound within your Sound.
So tell me again and again
    the golden code of these telling tales,
So I can hear you,
So I can really know.

Planting

These trees were pretty, delicate things,
    but you uprooted them all.
Do you hold a sack of seeds behind your back,
Or virgin land to plant again?
(I don't have a shovel, hoe, or money.)
Will you blow me away like golden seed
To grow in limitless fields?
I tell you if you water me I promise to grow,
And brighten all your days.

Eons

You raise your hand, my palm greets it,
Mirror-like.
You take a step, and I fall behind.
I wake to see breaking out of an egg a baby dragon,
But you correct me saying: *Baby Eagle.*

I'm like an echo drifting behind on the sand
Or blinking owl-like from stars above,
Waiting...waiting...to catch up to God.

Gift

On a blanket of waves on a floating bed
You carry me to a place where I meet I,
The insoluble bubble of Identity.
For years I've waited for this gift,
Its purpose unknown, the wrappings all but known –
You give and I take, I give and you take,
Like dueling lovers no one wins,
Until the day I really see
That what you are giving me, is me.

Nothing's Ever Lost

Nothing's ever lost,
It's in the Ocean,
Seen by invisible eyes,
Carried by invisible arms,
Preserved in invisible hearts –
In the blueness of the blue,
In the gold and white of the beach,
Where you took me up and kissed me.

Glory

You honor me, a human,
Like a stone submerged in water,
Mysterious and good.
I come to reason slower than the stone,
Though we're loved equally and gloriously the same.

You've sent me on a journey to discover truth
Through monstrous tides, again and again –
So I can see your Face in the water,
In the human, in the glory.

After Seeing the Film
In God's Hands

We pitched tar out of the bow and salt from the stern,
Moored her in the narrow straits that bordered
   on a great Peninsula.

Shell

What chapter are we on in this fairy tale?
You've woven fiction and fact throughout my story
Like life stubbing its toe on Truth and never apologizing.
I feel the current taking me out
And my hand can't reach yours,
And the ties that were home and affection are gone.
I'm your little conch, your sea animal,
Who begs to emerge from this tiny black spiral,
The little dark shell I've called home.

Consciousness Becoming the Form

Black veins becoming consciousness of the spider,
Beauty becoming consciousness of a queen,
A baby becoming the I AM.
Human speech becoming the inner voice,
The Blue Flower calling me Home.

Traveling

If one travels by cloud or by sole of a shoe,
What does does it matter?
One day you're riding in a boxcar with slaves,
The next day you're fighting off dogs,
The next day honored by colleagues.
We travel a trail only God knows, transfixed by a target:
Beyond death and the resurrection.

A Pilgrim's Progress

An elephant walk and dogs through a hoop,
Tightropes for viewing a circus of truth,
In how many mirrors and how many ways,
Can one venture the illusory way?

I prattled and pried and went out with the tide
In a boat on a stream in some stranger's dream
Until I awoke on some foreign soil,
Where water was smoke, and gold but oil.

Where am I? I cried to no one but me,
I'm done for, you see, but for the lie I flee,
No! I heard, from a Master named Z,*
You know all the secrets there are to be free!

I know little, alas, and cried many tears,
It's love that I seek – not doubt and not fear,
How far I've come on the journey thus far,
And all I have is my Self and that Star.

That Star shines aloft for you and your friends
Who travel so hard and seek but to mend,
Come here and see what surely will be
When you halt your steps and stand beside me.

I did as told and looked up at the sight
And behold I had none but the black and the night,
Then sudden it was that the light did shine,
Into heart and mind as if I'd been blind.

Then thundering there in the deepest of boughs
Was the laughter of God, and the mirth did grow
'Till all God's creatures were sounding the facts –
I wasn't lost, I had just lost the knack...

...the knack of being quiet and still,
Content and open and empty until
God's love streamed forth for the journey anew,
For all had come back to me, for You.

A circle of love was then complete,
I accepted the scars and lessons sweet
With a promise of Truth and that shining Star
Which approached so near, yet shone so far.

With God I'll journey the rest of my days
And discover the gold that rests inlaid
In footsteps which travel a path of thorns,
And sparkle like jewels in spite of the storm.

So guide me, try me, and I'll prove to be
Your tempered Soul who bears love for Thee
To some dark corner of these restless worlds --
With love, Divine Love, I am reborn.

* spiritual name of the current spiritual teacher

Colors

The secrets you gave me are like crushed stones
I grind into pigment – ochre, yellow, and blue.
I paint my portrait alongside yours,
    the most beautiful Secret.
The weight of crushed stones are like letters dissolved
In your holy stream: Life colored by the Word.

Soul

Moving silently and effortlessly,
Soul travels without marking its journey –
Invisible ink of the God Realm.

Unheard Music

My heart is a carrier for your Word to the Soul of the world,
My only possession, my entire life, is in your oceanic palm.

Your gaze (only) moves orchestras to fever pitch
With notes never heard before,
And the least of songs become unbounded,
Giving birth to musical winds, true fables of art and science.

With the Unheard Music, all the arts are single (now) –
They disappear together into a liquid mirror of God.

Joy

The hand of God has touched me
Restoring an old friendship with joy,
Like a bee that zooms straight to the flower
Or an architect who builds a house full of windows.
How quickly I pass through the veils
Of joy and sorrow, riches and loss
To love You more than I ever have before –
To be a sun that keeps shining,
To be a moon that keeps reflecting that Sun!

Listening

Your Light contains many kinds of light,
But I see only what I'm ready for.
In the *Shariyat*, the Book of Light,
What do I really hear?
There are many tones hidden in the octave,
I see the whitest shade of white, dazzling the lily
And the unheard treble note opening the rose.
Now I'm listening to the center of myself, where listening is,
And consciousness IS.

Eternal Friendship

Launching their journeys so long ago,
Two made their way up river –
Captains of their lives and honor,
They arrived at God's wide port –
Then entered the Glittering City.

After Emily Dickinson

Four walls – Empyrean –
With the strangest view –
Then I – four cornered –
Chained – away it flew –
Into clear circumference
Looking on the gem's façade –
He cut the glass so clearly –
And saw what God already knows.

Scroll

A scroll unwinds in my belly,
You read me from the inside out.
No longer am I the exterior girl
Who reads books for answers
Or dreams too long about a question.
You pour molten God stuff into my heart
And my mind revolts with loving kindness.
A celestial alphabet is talking back between my shoulders,
My entire body is writing with your pen!

Meeting

Blue eyes and daffodils,
Meet me in the garden at eight,
We have a union scheduled.
You'll come from behind the weeping willow
    and surprise me,
I'll hide in the gentian bush expecting summer
    to last all year long –
Your auburn hair is reckless, but I trust you.
Sweep the garden with your long tunic
And worship at my feet the simple daisies of being.
Master of my life, I pray you meet me tonight,
My fragrance is in the air only for you.

Music Box

A box of music arrived,
I'll open it before it closes.
Inner ears unseal the corners,
But my heart seals them up again.
Mine is a love that travels in both direction:
Just open the box!

Free

One day I became the idolater of my Self,
Other idols crashed around me brass-horned, then silent.
To think I gave my money and best possessions to these things!
How could a bribe beget grace? It was like a false religion,
Power swept into corners like dust and offered up like treasure.
What is Real? That was the question that broke the spell,
Banished it to a far corner with iron gods kneeling –
Shadows dissolving in a noonday sun.

Horizon

A new vista appears on the horizon
Illuminating the great plain of God –
Only Soul can travel as far as the heart can see.
The mind's physicist throws up his greedy hands
Not comprehending the ungraspable law of love.
Divided by nothing love stands the sum of all,
Shimmering in the river-fed country of Light and Sound
Soul listens to Silent Home –
Over the ridge, just so far,
Over the next horizon.

Constellation

Gods coast up and down the stars
Calling me on crystal frequencies.
My forehead slips into the Big Dipper,
My eyes shine like liquid stars,
A galaxy hangs from five fingers,
And my head is wrapped in the arms of Jupiter.
Atom, cell, molecule of light –
All constellations of possibility,
Beyond this black celestial bowl of Earth.

Landscape

Giant hands of the oak,
Seeds blowing on the ripening field,
Rocking the world in a vociferous green,
Steady the roots, lovely the pale,
Halcyon feather trembling in the nest.

Becoming

I'm no longer my father's daughter,
The child who begged for love and sweets.
My Teacher taught me that when I walk in his footsteps
The only place I am is forever young.

I join those beings who love secrets best,
Buried in tomes of light on spiritual mountains
Where holy bibles are found in foothills of sound
And words scatter ancient fences like so much breath.

I know what I'm becoming, I'll be what you dreamed,
I'm moving through the doorway to new Life.

Wishes

Let me see so clearly in the Light of your love
    that I have no illusions.
Let me move with such speed into the Sound
    that I cast no shadows.
Let me speak with such Truth to those who wish to hear
    that I always have a gift to give.
Let me act so boldly in the name of the Mahanta*
    that I have all my tomorrows to love You.
Let my dreams be so golden and daring
    that I'm forever a part of your vision.
Let me fly so high to see the glory of Life
    that I truly know how to live!

* the Godman who gives spiritual liberation

Dialogue

An alphabet of lies circles the globe,
Don't listen to it!
Listen to the star that flies from the orbit of Love,
Be free!

Love to your heart's content and drink of Me:
Star dust in the crown of creation,
Dew slipping in between fingers of flowers,
A filament beneath the ocean lighting the shark's lure,
Footholds on spiritual mountains,
    beyond human comprehension.

The feathers on your arms are like eagles' wings,
Tired of your disguise, come be with Me.
Let Me love you for who you are,
Sacred – One – Beaming,
Flying into the lap of azure brightness into the heavens,
Carrying My love to the multitudes.

Vase

I asked, "How can I receive the wisdom of God?"
You said: "Look at this vase. It's clear,
With a spiral on its face, empty as the day is long.
When empty it's filled with the invisible,
With flowers, it's filled with the visible.
So be like a spiral on the face of life – clear, cut,
Flowers blooming."

Commuting the Sentence

When you tell me of places so high,
Bathed in mysterious blue and soundless sound,
Do you believe I can walk there with nothing to catch my fall?
Nothing remains but to fly there –
Your call is too strong for this human heart.
My whole body is like ripe fruit
    opening to a rush of silver wind,
HU* commutes the stories of my lives to high seas
    and mountain air,
Like first and last breaths, like brilliant cut flowers in a vase.

* a sacred sound coming from the heart of God

Love Lost and Found

I traveled my love like a river
In a boat that was made for just two,
And everyone else was traveling
And seeing this love but you.

Can I ever forget the freedom
That comes and goes like waves,
I'm one, then two, then one once again
In a dream I once dreamed with you.

Love is an ocean and the body a boat
Can I help it if they're one and the same?
Love is a woman and an ocean remote
But endless water – like love – remains.

It's easy to move into the heart of God
Now that I am the Alone,
For wherever a heart once beat true,
There God finds a true companion.

Alchemy

Currents ebb and flow
About the circumference of a whirlpool,
The entrance to my heart.

You arrived on the captain's ship, slipping on rocks,
Pretending to be the lone wolf,
Appearing like a moon in the dark escorted by sleepers
Who left their bodies to accompany you
    on far-flung hairs of the sun,
Burning and sifting in the eyeglass of space,
    the door of my heart.

Gold is made at the edges of your eyes,
Their snowy ellipses slide back onto Arcturus,
Bending around again up my sleeve and into my throat,
Launching words that turn ash to silver: I love you.

Friends long gone have come around again in a boat
    with the Captain,
Singing songs every heart should know.
Your face is like a lotus crowning all the blessings of the Master.
The Master – you and I – why, when?
The answers are leading me,
And where I go, I shall find them.

Fifth Initiation

Now I'm in the book of Love –
I saw my name in gold,
The Mahanta* signed the page and wrote:
"This is all there is –
One Soul marked for the Godhead in this lifetime."
Spoken and read – my name:
Soul.

* * *

This ocean is so vast,
I only have the sail of my own being, wind and water.
The sirens that called to me are silent,
The destination is the deep,
This destination is not final,
This journey is the Sea of Seas,
I am walking barefoot on the sea.

* the Light Giver

Silver Circle

Blown into a silver circle on one ringing note,
A Master who looked like a god said:
"Light has just begun in this kingdom of giants
Where the body has no fortune and truth is not lies."
I speak your name in this blue land, on a white road I am –
Advancing to the Bourchakoun.*

* a group of spiritual adepts, the Ancient Order of the Vairagi

Karma

Dinosaurs, witches and bogeymen –
The citizenry of Mars, Pluto and Atlantis
In the last days of forgetfulness,
Czars of rank and pompous feuding,
Turned in beds of deep water
Never to be heard from again:
Now I'm hearing them again,
Crying *Mahanta! Oh Mahanta!**

* one who can give spiritual liberation

Blue Map

A treasure house possessed a treasure chest,
But a pirate came and stole it all.
I got another map – blue with blue ribbon –
Tied by one who knows directions:
Ocean to the right and forest to the left,
Desert above and swamp below –
Where to go?
I looked for a path, searched and found:
The compass was in my heart and the sound in my head –
Not in Paris, the streets, or Khartoum.

Space / Time

"Where are we going?" I asked.
"Close your eyes and carry a tune," you said.
And then we were Everywhere.

Nowhere is in the heart of the mind,
So carry your heart into whiteness,
There and everywhere: IT exists beyond the stars.
"I will show you something of tomorrow,
For the destiny of this earth is to become a Sun."

Bindu*

Cascading down a silver branch I hear a call
From the leaf-tipped prodigy of spirit-men,
The answer to everything I've ever known –
A seed sound, righteous seedling in a forest of flowers,
Raised in the light of Sugmad's* glory.

I am the Son, he is the Father,
I am the Daughter, he is the Beloved.
This is it! I am born!
A happy blue bird flies in my ear, I am gone!

In a meadow of blue flowers I'm feeding on God,
This blue is the end of the world.
I'm cascading down a river of silver
That divides the Two Worlds.
I hold my breath, yet I have no breath,
I am here, yet not here,
In the blue, cascading blue!

* a spiritual seed sound that assists with spiritual growth
* another name for God

Blue Heron

I was a king-fisher once,
Blue stalks yielding in white water.
Then ice came in winter,
I knew a greater catch would come.
I swam and soared
And settled down (again).
I was a blue heron (now)
Seeking refuge in a clime
Of a bevy of birds waiting for a chance
To eat the food of wishes,
The eternal food beyond fishermen's nets:
To be a heron in the net of love,
In deep water.

The Ancient One

The ancient structure tilts and swoons.
Who is it at my door?
The Adept one, the conqueror,
The enamored one who holds
For me a mirror and breaks it
Into a thousand cities of rhapsody
   and waters.
This is the end of my beginning,
The shooting of stars has just begun.
This is the end of the falling of moons,
And suns in the distance.
I will wear a cloak of fortune
In the guise of him who steers me on
To the door of sundry loves and kisses.
I am the one most searched for:
A lonely heart in a sea of claims.

Garden

The King is in the garden
And flowers are known
By the scent of love.
The ones I've picked
Are the roses of that One:
Light of impenetrable Sound.
I am a song in the heart of him
Who burns five flowers in a flame.

What is in This Desert?

The sand of God blows into the mirror of being.
Sand is a caravan, and caravans are travelers
Racing to the heart of the mountain,
Of obsidian or chalk, I can't remember now.
I am Soul, a fruit-maker,
The wreath and garland of Sugmad's* works
Doing the bidding of the least of servants
    and weary travelers.
I have seven shoes: two for Soul,
And five for everything I've left behind.
I'm not lost, I know where the wind blows:
It blows from the Mountain.

* another name for God

Karma Resolved

The merry stones I threw across the brook
Have landed at my feet, glistening like stalwart soldiers.
One sailed over a river and across the ocean,
One past this universe, and again landed at my feet.
Red, orange, gilt-blue and yellow-worn,
They pile up to my head – this silver head –
Beaming signals to shore,
In the burning sea of this loving heart.

Two Souls Meet After A Long Time

Marvelous sister!
Of this peace it can be said in the singing book
We are two Souls old in the world,
Having met again in wonderful communion.
On what shore did we last meet –
Greece, France, some monsoon island?
Having met again, we build now in the house of HU* --
The keystone left of a golden arch
And love, an old password.
In the dome of God, love sounds north, south, east, and west –
And though I have no direction and you have no name for it,
I love you.

* a sound emanating from the heart of God that sustains all creation

It Breaks Upon the Ocean

It breaks upon the ocean,
The rainbow above a ship,
Shining from the heart of the sea.

We are able-bodied swimmers,
Wave upon wave in this Golden Age
When hundreds of ships will come to moor,
And carry melodious swimmers
To all points on God's earth.

Orison

This body has become an orison of sound:
    Drums in my belly,
    Flutes playing down my back,
    Bells in my eyes,
    Legs coursing with the ocean's roar.
I'm singing – body and Soul –
Flying into bright sheets of music
Where sight is real and destiny sounds in twelve tones.
Dare I dream to become an instrument of God?
I dare to become an instrument of God:
I am deftly played for music in the worlds.

Freedom

Up from cloud day breaks,
Up from Soul day dawns,
The wind blows,
And this day is Eternity.
At the foot of the mountain
I meet my Master, and he is me.
Can I go any further than this?
I have longed for this win for centuries –
Wreath around my neck, and a smile on my face.
There are no words,
And we love until there is no more time,
This love has no bounds and leaves no trail.
By the divine Light and Sound
I have left every original home
To fly to this happy mountain
And be with you at this hour,
On the day of my deliverance,
From clouds.

Warrior's Alphabet

Atoms are spinning in my heart,
And spiral out to the ends of this universe
(Abelene...Ansio...Atma...)
This is everything I am:
The rest is anything I can't conceive.

If I take up a sword I've already failed,
The work having already been done by Sugmad.*
Is this what it means to be a servant –
To know, hear, and be still?

Everything sounds in the heart of the sea,
Everything champions its own Being: A...B...C...D.
I am an atom spinning in the worlds,
I've heard the sound of Z.*

* another name for God
* spiritual name of the current spiritual teacher of Eckankar

Architect of HU

A giant mason being my father and his father before that
(My inheritance being this statue of grief),
Dissolved giant stones in smoke and thunder
Revealing a new Temple in quartz and light
Shining as one – golden – vibrating – room:
Where worlds travelled from the navel of a Great One –
A Being I knew millennia ago,
The hammering travelling up and down heart strings,
Rising and falling the length of a spiral to God and back again,
Sounding there one – vibrating – note:
Building perfect ratios,
Building God.

Message from the Angel of Love
During a Dark Night

This journey you so aptly describe as bountiful
Is a saga of wars,
A well-tuned mayhem and slaughter
Of the lower self.

To become one,
Yield up your Soul to the great one,
And become more like the Great One,
Knowing you are serving God, *Baraka Bashad!**

There's no end to the journey,
And though none are cheering for you
As you pass the milestone,
Be of good cheer and hold your head high,
Because a Golden Heart wins all races,
Won and lost forever.

Sound rises to a fever pitch in your head and glands,
Be not afraid – it is God making you less mortal.
With eyes you'll see morning,
In your heart you'll know what Eternity is,
All for keeping one lonely sigh in the heart of God.

* Persian: *May the blessings be!*

True Marriage

If I asked what it would take to do such a thing,
You'd say it will take a thousand years,
And I'd say I'm willing to give up everything,
And you'd say, *Maybe*.

I turn silver and round like lights in infinity,
And hear a thousand stars of Spirit singing:
You are with me, gold and silver together –
And much more than this!

Past Lives

Spread out before me like a fan –
Rooms in a room, in this room.
A Chinese queen catches Japanese moths,
In this house, many rooms, big dreams.

A golden roof is built by a King,
The Chinese queen can't catch Japanese moths forever –
There's more light than ever and no rooms whatsoever
When dreams are built by a King.
The King and I will leave this house!

Earth

A man in the street and the dog over there,
That child and that woman –
Are messages of deliverance
From the everyday creed of guile and cunning.
In the dome of Earth hearts beat
The simplest measure of God's song.
Common men are love songs at my door,
On this beautiful little planet Earth.

A Visit with Kal Niranjan*

The Doctor of Sloth came to me and said,
"You're not feeling well?
Come with me, and I'll show you a good time."
So we looked down a well,
And I saw a mirror, and the mirror was black.
And he said, "You've come a long way, so drink!"
"I'll never drink from this pitch," I said.

"You will, or you will never know peace."

"I don't want peace, I want the glory of God!"

"Then look again in the water."

And I saw the masks of mummies,
And the caretakers of the dead and others,
I saw the murder of my own life and havoc,
And piteous people and catastrophe.

Then I slept and dreamed:
I was growing in the House of God,
But no one watered me, a lowly vegetable in the ground.
A little girl came to me and said,
"I am the daughter of darkness grown old,
As this universe works in reverse –
What is dark becomes light,
What is hateful becomes love,

Welcome to the Land of Two."
I said, "But there is only One."

And she said, "Follow me."

So I went into a labyrinth
And it wound around and around again,
And it came to nothing, and nothing I was.

Then out of the place of no-thing IT sang,
The music of millennia burned in my ears,
And a Heart of Hearts said I was love only.
"How can this be?" I asked.

"You know no shame," cried Niranjan.
"Accept your Self, and I must cast you out,
So go!"

And I went –
I went Home.

* The negative force that governs the lower worlds

Love Story

If you could hear me with ears that aren't stone
And a heart that's not clay, I could tell you
That our story is in a golden book
And it will be told to us
In the most poetic way,
Not by chance, and not by luck,
But by the grace of love
That each has for the other.

Neck, lips, eyes, hair and body songs
Clean me on the battleground of desire.
Hoodwinked and let down,
I rise up again and face you as I would myself,
In the large way that warriors do.

Men Walking in the Face of God

The sun and the earth isn't at your command,
But your heart is your command
To wage love on an invisible enemy.
Without the enemy you are lost,
Not knowing where the war is.
There's no plan for victory,
Because strife remaining in the ranks
Is only a lessening of forces.

I want to see the Face and slay the giant sleeping –
The righteous among us,
Who see a ferret in the face of the poor
And a monster in the eye of the sun.
This is a holiday from fear,
So I am picking up the sword.

I will not always be dead or asleep
Carrying dust in the bowels of time.
For I am walking toward the sun,
I am traveling for the Ancient One.

Red Door

I've opened and shut it a thousand times,
    this portal of desire.
Who can know the comings and goings of ghosts
Who spring to my side over thousands of years,
Over thousands and thousands of years?
The Master knows!

Spiritual Eye

Serpentine jewel,
The lotus within my heart
Is as starry-eyed as your Face,
Shining like a mirror in the sea.
What shells do you carry in each hand?
They are the ears and eyes of my heart.
In the sand of forgetfulness they shine like Two Beauties,
In a single Eye of Dawn.

Spiritual Invitation

Be my guest, my poor one,
Who goes among the roads.
Palter for a penny, a wise one,
Who takes the gross for penitence
And the last of coins for a silver purge.
It is I, a Task:
For the Masters have said well
That where'er I pay,
All payments come to naught,
And forever will.

Light

I.

As many colors as there are, there are as many kinds of love. Tears shed in the search for Love have burned a series of infinitesimal color wheels around my heart for centuries. No vegetable, mineral, human or animal assuaged the swelling and receding tides of color that consumed me finally in Black, or the absorption of all colors in flames of endurance. This is the weight of the heart. And just as blood turns black when it seeks the air, so did the Love of my life. The Love of my life being that stronghold of mirth and devotion devoted to the Spirit of this world and worlds I could not fathom.

II.

The wheel of Fortune is a colorful wheel around which flies a boundary incessantly. This is the limitation of ardor or Desire. Around the houses of this wheel fly pictures of yearning. Yearning constitutes the actions of the heart after its Maker, and desire constitutes the actions of the Will after its gratifications. These are houses of the holy or the 12 spheres of action on mind and matter throughout eternity. The colors of the houses are aspects of fortune, and when seen together whirling about a circumference, are aglow with a fiery brilliance. This is the heart of the matter, or the Light of Soul. Its visage is a colored cloak of Fortune which it wears while sojourning in the physical worlds. To don this cloak is the actor's privilege and protection. To cast it off is his birthright, and to assume the white light of creation is where he lives throughout eternity. So one might say that in every event in life and death there is color, and that in both life and death there is Light.

III.
White light shines forth in a star. Where does it not shine? It shines in hell, in the eyes of the blind, and the hearts of the weary. It shines at the foot of a mountain gilded with pearls, tears of the aged. The pipers call it a mad song. The weavers call it the incessant dark of dread things to come. The masters call it wisdom notes heard in the heart of matter. Though it is called by many names, it is the aftermath of living things. When the hour descends, a call is heard by those who have seen the Sun in all its glory. By earth, air, fire and water the spectrum ceases to be in the full glory of its round. That spectral wheel called the Mask of Fortune is dead and lights the most privy of lights – the aging and deathless Sun at the heart of everything that lives. This is the Light that lives, born in the heart of the dark where it rises to seek all color, or the Flame of Happiness.

HUE

BLACK is a diadem of faith.

RED is a nomad seeking refuge in a fire, albeit the lost
yielding to no one.

ORANGE is the infidelity and praise of all things made
in the image of God.

YELLOW is a consummation of an everlasting fire of grief,
a sapphire of storms.

GREEN is the door on which a comely one hangs,
staggered by the grace of forgiveness.

BLUE is a refuge sought by birds whose eyes resolve
in a locus of chance, a madness fit.

INDIGO is the tip of flame that meets a tongue of love
stripped bare of words and incantations.

VIOLET is a robe incarnate adorning the backs of saviors,
whose speech pierces the whole rainbow, arc upon arc.

WHITE is the comforter, scheme and enigma
on which creaturehood is scaffolded.

There is Nothing Compared to God's Love

If you hold on to a tree
To save yourself from flying away,
He will uproot the tree.

If you thirst for water
He'll teach you to dig a well
And search for the mouth of a river.

If you crave the womb,
He'll give you a thousand births.

If you desire the beloved,
He'll test your five hearts.

There is nothing compared to God's love.

Divine Desire

A flame, spire, circle, a lovely moon
All obeyed your command,
Blowing me around the course of this universe:
This is love.

Take me to the frontier, to the middle of boiling sea –
I sleep but am awake,
I dream but do not sleep.
Take me onto the lap of nothingness,
Into the arms of creation.
I am yours in the heat, in the heart,
In thunder and lightning on the high Sea,
Inside this dream of divine desire.

Spiritual Brotherhood

The incarnation of the Brotherhood
Is like a rope of knotted wind,
Beams of light on the whitest of sails
Flying on the trinity of my heart.
I am your face and yours is mine –
Delicate, leading like a boatswain
Who hurls his oars aloft
With the hope that the sea will benefit,
And we will be made whole as others who sail after us,
Into the Cosmic Sea.

Next Step

If I knew it I would take it,
Say it or dream it:
I just am.

It's the song I don't know,
The book I don't know,
And what is the name?
I'm neither intelligent nor stupid,
I just am.

Standing in the fountain of perennial knowledge,
With wisdom and the curtain drawn,
I know you are on the other side,
Just waiting for me.

Atlas: Snow and Ice
(Moving to Minnesota)

What a delectable morsel,
This sheet of crystalline pie,
Native ground to those who arrived
Speaking a language of the North Wind.

Here heat is released in the limbs of spiritual runners
Who make tracks with speed and lightness,
To teach wisdom in the future days,
In the sunny mass that lies ahead.

Spring is eternal here,
So come take the cold in your arms,
Melt it in the furnace of your heart,
Your two legs leaping over the Mississippi.

Silver Rain

The desert is in bloom,
Blue hyacinth and marigold,
Rivers running in pairs like gold blonde things,
Reflecting a lover's moon.

Knighting the night of paradise
In the afterglow of showers,
The Divine Presence moves,
Searing Soul with silver soundings.

Golden Wisdom Temple*

I invite you, wondrous Soul, to enter in!
A celestial clock is striking
And the music you've always heard
And mistook for the noise of the world
Is the golden ringing aperture of heaven.

Listen to the age-old beat of rising hearts,
Your deathless state of being in the Lamakan,*
Lakes and forest about your windy hair,
The tresses of Eden stirring on your head.

* * *

Where are you?
In an orbit around the sun or biding your time in the belly of wishes?
If you ride an animal long enough you begin to resemble it
Having not the strength to dismount and walk,
  carrying your own burden.
Rings of planetary waves are like hunger
  drawing you back to the source,
Like food for the pale Soul who has walked and walked...

Who are you?

900,000 universes are waiting for the Master –
Wearing flesh, skin or scales, does it matter
To the heart who knows the coming of spring
  without seasons or clothes?

Look within,
Even for the pale imitation of goods delivered to your door,
Because knowing begins with faith and you will know him,
He who knows you.

How are you?

A towering spire spills your song to the wind,
And the wind whistles down the middle of an adorned road
Matching the Master's gait.
Even flowers are reeling from the Sound,
And pilgrims who never knew they were
Plant their feet firmly at the gates of HU.*

* * *

If all life were set on the head of a pin
And Jupiter, the stars, Mercury and Venus
Sat in the lap of a dust mite
The glory of God would be the same:
In the large and small,
In the light, from the light.

You are good and worthy
Even if you don't know the Name.
It can be caught without effort –
No prizes to win, no contest to enter,
No better or best, consume or be consumed.
Lie down, close the traps of the mind
And open the world of your heart,
The heart of your world,
And wish for what you've always wished for
In the deep dark pearl dawn of you, and speak:

Welcome the greatest Teacher.

The king and queen of Heaven reside here,
In the town squares and ghettos –
Light the lamps in Peoria and the dung well in Macon,
The flood will come, it is all the same to eyes that see,
The face of Love within, though hiding.

Come out! Come out!

Exit your old house in costumes or rags,
With head coverings or feathers,
With grins or toothless masks.
Carry your hunted head and arrow,
One to give away and the other to find your way –
You don't have to speak – longing is enough.
Listen to IT,
Its name is your name,
You were born at different times
But the address is the same,
The prize already won.
Surrender and wave the white flag of your heart
And give it to Him,
He will burn it, He is your friend,
You are loved.
Come with me, an army of Lovers,
Drawn by the Light of Lights to the Heart of Hearts,
On a path where you find everything!

* Golden Wisdom Temple - located in Chanhassen, Minnesota; there are
others in the spiritual worlds
* Lamakan - the spiritual region of the endless or eternal
* HU - the voice of God

Spiritual Destiny

The thunder in my heart
Is the spring of a recurring dream,
The diamond beam of love
Is focused to such heat and fusion
That I am barely alive,
Wanting to die to everything
That is not me in you.

Help me to see beyond the dream,
What is left to build in this eon of time
In the Soul of imaginings,
To bear the love of you,
To build Love for you
In all things and sing –

This is my wish:
To know, be at the heart of It,
To have, love and fly
    to the highest arc of creation,
To give all, for it is my destiny:
Take me, and show me thy Truth!

Sea Travel

Into another octave we fly,
To hear the sequel of a love fest,
Deranged, ecstatic and danceable.
Secrets lie upon the staff,
And the treble clef hides meaning
That bears me forward on your laughing wave.
Show me your secrets, your loving gaze,
So I can bridge the gulf
Between me and resurrection in the Sea world,
With its deep currents and mighty songs
Singing across the ocean floor,
Emerging from the salt of my countless, laughing tears.

Contemplation

Everything is within me, shining ocean to shining ocean,
A liquid diamond of identity without end –
Stars, planets, and a multitude of universes too!
I could be a light on any of them to serve the majesty
    that is the Mahanta.*
I'm a microcosm to your macrocosm,
Sounding lightning and thunder –
A Soul whose only name is *Love in Eternity*,
With no ending or beginning, just the Light of Lights
And the sound of Soul, Its music vibrating
    in the creation of God,
Forever yours in the glory of the *Infinite Life* –
Mine to be and mine to give as Soul,
Who loves and is here for no other reason than this,
Sent as your messenger in the worlds – to who knows where –
A part of the great and happy mystery:
    the thrill of deep living, sharing and unspeakable bliss.
What is life? It is Soul in Its bliss, in Its action,
In Its contemplation, in Its service to the golden heart
Of the Mahanta of all worlds.

* a matrix for the Light and Sound of God

Love and Friendship

You
Who the Master sent to me on angels' wings
Starred like a silent sentinel in the dark,
     graded wood of my journey –
Do you know why you came here?
Do you know why I have come?
It was meant that we know each other.
Let's take the fruit of our beginnings
And the root of our forgetfulness,
Placing them in the rich soil of companionship,
And grow ourselves into a field of Freedom.

Gold

The oven and the baker,
The candle and the taper,
What's betwixt them is the One,
Gold dividing and multiplying again.
By and by,
I will be the bread you eat,
The light you see by.
In the flame I see you,
In the heat I rise, a miracle,
All the way to rainbow's end.

Empire Builder

(The eagle told me to hide nothing,
What's left over from the hunt
Will be used to build a nest.
On the tundra it's safe to say
No man dwells here, save him who means to stay.)

Lucky charms and four-leaf clovers
Have no meaning here,
For luck does not abound in the wild
Where the heart roams to be caught
By the wind and wind only:
It's an intentional thing.

I've built an empire in my dreams,
Wide vision and hope strung to
     the ballast of Soul,
And set them aloft on a mast of creation,
With the indelible stamp of stars above,
Imprinting my heart with the songs of great Sailors.

I navigated material waters and found them dull,
Those which brought Columbus to his knees
And the fisher-kings who stole from those
     they begged from,
Now lost at the bottom of the sea.

I'm captain and servant of this ocean vessel,
No more, no less –
Beholden to a queen who rules beneath my breast.
The empire I dream has no country, yet binds all in union,
The empire I live in boasts not of power,
But kindly deeds in excess of asking.
All this flourishes on a quicksand of being
And is mine, as long as I relinquish it for the All.

Orchestra

I like this company of players:
The tuba ringing out laughs,
The drum beating out the ages,
Singers lifting me with joyous flights of fancy,
A cymbal splashing love into aisles,
A conductor who makes his way
Level-headed to the end:
Touching the face of God,
Coda after coda, birth after birth, loud and soft,
Accompanying lives.

Venusian Song

Perishable locks and planetary stays,
The bonds that bind will not remain for long.
A contract emerges centuries old
Not from a farmer or industrialist bold
But from starry-eyed benefactors
With whom we remain in love.
Love is the planet and love is the world
To which we are going with hearts like pearls –
Not by spacecraft and not by boat
Or through telescopic lens – it's less remote.
Hail fellow travelers! Have I seen you somewhere?
In my dreams, in your fields, I could swear you were there.
The minute I wake up I see what you mean,
When the heavens roll back, it's all very plain
That the man with the plan and the Masters that be
Are real and with us, linking us up in Eternity.

Harvest

Several moons have risen and fallen,
At my back door the sun has risen,
And far beyond the gate I remember
The teeth of hounds – but no more.

Pumpkins and apples spill out on the floor,
Seeds into fledgling fruits,
Births and births and births,
Resuscitating to make room for more,
But no more.

A swan has sailed on who won't come back,
Like this Soul who won't return
To a thousand continents, dying to make more –
But no more.

My heart has grown a straight edge
Past the white heart that gave it birth.
I, too, will become a Master,
More than this I cannot offer,
These are the gifts of the humble earth I was –
But no more.

Diamond

A head – a crown where brain used to sit –
Like jewels talking to one another
Slipping up and down vertebrae,
Steely necklaces draping the worshipper in me.
The light is now fathomless, I am lost in it,
Burning is not a question, I am used to it,
I have another skin called *eternal*.
Fire travels slowly, then quickly like a kiss
Blowing across a plain of pain,
To the high sphere where cities received a new resident,
A true citizen who crossed the moat of forgetfulness
And entered a diamond light – her light reign.

Letter to an Eagle

You are familiar as dawning day,
A recollection as simple as walking.
Just by the act of seeing, you ratify for me a treaty
Created inside a whirling wind of golden wings
Fanning existence into a screaming white heat.

In a zone where none breathes air as refined
You gaze upward to the crowning point beyond
The cliff where I've stopped to yearn and know –
Can I touch the cloak of Being? Can I wear the mantle too?
Let me fly with you!

Destiny in Ocean

Let's pick up the pieces of our hearts then –
One, two, ten, one million,
Scattered on the bed of the ocean of time.
The sea is chiseled into bone, shell and glass
And breaks open sunken treasures that fishes have made home –
So out of the boundary waters and into the Sun!
Dredge up the salt furies, caskets and barrels of oil,
For now we ride the tides of insurgence
To a paradise planet of God-lovers,
Tropical and lush with spiritual heat,
The divers are all going Home.
Are these the sunken gems you carried when you were
    a tourist of civilization?
Is this the captain's table where our families ate
    until they forgot their names?
Now we fly into ethereal waters
That nourished the silt bed from millennia ago,
Rushing out of moorings to pull the rusted anchor up
To sail to heaven, shores of angels, and You.

The Dream Just Is

I was once an Emperor,
Do you remember me?
I used to tear down cities and rebuild them
By the sweat of others,
Then I learned the lesson of sweet humility.

I was once a Mother,
Do you remember me?
Daughters and sons – I gave them all –
My milk, my bread,
And learned the lesson of responsibility.

I used to be a Soldier,
You might remember me,
I conquered towns and cities
With the blood of my brothers,
And learned the lesson of great adversity.

I used to be a Madman,
No one remembers me,
I walked the streets despairing
No one would ever find me,
A caravan of one circling the globe
Looking for One who might see me.

I used to be a Disciple,
Sitting at the guru's feet,
Wandering roads like a spiritual child,
Begging for alms and casting off family
Until I found I was lost, to me.

I used to be a Poet turning a musical phrase,
Capturing the image of God
On the white of a simple page,
Then learned the face of God was in me.

Now I place a keystone in the house of God,
Let me set this stone in place,
Let us set these stones in place,
For the dream just is!

With no place to go except the heart of God,
The dream of Mastership is all I ever wanted,
That truth may utter changeless and through the ages sing,
To scatter Love like golden stars, for this is all there is.

A Reason to Live

Life, the enduring miracle,
The burning ribbon with which gifts are tied,
A glass for which water's poured,
The gaze of freedom for which we travel so far,
    so lightly.

Signposts say how far we've walked,
    not what the journey is about.
That is for me to say –
That is for us, sacred travelers, to know.

Distance exists only in the heart,
And the rate of travel is measured by the learning days.
As the Mahanta* is always with me knowing the journey I take,
I will open the gift and see my life, in the living.

* the Light Giver

Lost

Which body am I?
I'm lost in a sea of knowing:
My eyes, your head, my heart, your breath.
If I stay here I have no address,
But I'll never go astray if I live in the heart of the Sea.
The Sea, its body, its love,
Is where I come from, who I am, where I go.

Looking Ahead (3051)

The year sparkles in the glass,
Purple, yellow and emerald,
A spiritual kiss on the mouth of the Alone,
In this year of ascension.

I could be a star in the New World,
Or go to the valley below
And be with those who seek the living water –
For thousands of years they've thirsted for it.

These are my brothers since 1990,
As the world proclaimed a new calendar and calibration,
A future of stars, love, and contentment.
I will drink the whole cup,
Advancing to a hierarchy of knowing
And blessed by sounds for which there is no echo,
In this, our galactic draught.

Take my hand and close it around the goblet,
Make your stand under a calliope of spiritual colors,
Sense lightning in the jungle of space-time,
Between Andromeda and the star shape of your heart.

Here we stand on the star deck of Soul
Wishing everyone was here,
As silver fires move over the ancient wings of expert archers
Bearing songs of the Vairagi* and pealing sounds of laughter,
In Love's dances of the moment.

* spiritual adepts, the Ancient Order of the Vairagi

Course

All courses lead to the ocean,
All rivers run their course to the One.
My mother, brothers, sisters,
All the byways and hidden ways:
Do I not constitute the family of your heart singing this Song –
And the hunger to know the intimate spiritual relation?
I want to have all the lessons,
Teach the music of your love in this classroom,
So we might repair all the water ways,
All the hidden channels to your Ocean.

Family Tree

I searched for you, Mahanta,* like kin.
Though you are not my father, mother or brother,
The spiritual blood that runs in you runs in me,
Like the sap of an ancient tree
That grows an entire forest of seedlings.

You are the ancient root of my spiritual youth.
The Mahanta's ways are the vine,
A spiritual lineage flows from your eyes to mine,
Your leaves shimmering in the heart of love.

The primordial Mahanta flows among flowers of the field,
As Souls scatter among the four winds of earth and planets –
The Brothers who came and went,
Members of the Mahanta's spiritual family
Who lost and gained their inheritance again.

The primordial Mahanta is like heartwood,
Glorious root in sacred ground.
One hundred trees are as one tree, one tree is as a million,
In the forest of the Brothers of the Leaf.

* the Light Giver

Secret

You tell me a daring secret:
I am who I am.

You polish this bronze head,
Siphon off the remaining oil,
Twist copper filaments in my ears,
Now harmony burns like fire in two eyes,
I hear you: *I believe the whispers of God.*

The future is already a city,
The present already a garden,
The past is but a low white plain of forgiveness.

I am that which is called home,
I am she who carries an infinite tune,
I am he who speaks to anyone who will listen,
The secret is out: *I am Love only.*

Straight and Narrow

I say to you go lightly
I say to you don't shout
The work is done in silence
And I will help you out.

The only thing that matters
Is a God given plan
To bring you to the ninth step*
Of creation in the man.

You absolve to be holy
You absolve to be free
But the thing that's most important
Is to see yourself in Me.

Everything is sacred
And everything is calm
In your heart lie all the answers
Like a healing balm.

Give your cares to the Light
And your worries to the Sound
For all that lies for you in wait
Is just waiting to be found.

The song you sing is clearest
When it leaves your weary head
And enters into the heart of things
Love is all it says.

The greater vision that you seek
Is already in your view
Just stand upon your own two feet
For what you see is You.

* when one becomes a co-worker with God

Afternoon in Cornwall

The elegant sea,
The way the tree pairs with the root,
The easing of all pain.
 Here I stand in light of the dance,
 Throwing joy, seeking after nothing,
 No one.
I alone (tree alone),
In green grass fibers and roots of your Being,
Glass-gold like palominos,
The crescent sun and moon filtered like braids,
Like prayers.
Bear me forward through the atomic curtain of God –
The cornfield blossoms of youth,
The music beating wind with joy in your field.
 I am standing, root-standing,
 Ever-green, never-ending,
Blue-green ever abandoning my rough land,
To your blue Sea.

Seven Seas

In the basin of the Nile I was your supplicant,
In the freezing bay I was your messenger,
In the legion of the Pacific I was silent,
Overcome by a flood.
Wherever I am in this body with changing face, I will love –
To learn the elastic measure of human happiness and error:
Offer the heart, and offer it!

In the seven seas of the God realm
I was a child who ate salt and saw fishes,
Until your face swam before me like a swan.
In the crater lake of the moon and rock pools of Saturn,
My body became like water filtering back your silver Sea.

I am becoming what you promised,
An ocean filling up the seven seas of my heart,
Flooded by what you promised.

E K *

Chains and stones, rudimentary links,
A fence – no, a gate to God I made,
The only route I knew:
Footpaths and stepping stones,
I walked them all.

Then a bluebird sang "forever" in a day,
Chirped worlds inside an atom,
And in me You stood,
Foundation of my being, temple of my heart,
Lady of my Soul: EK.

* an ancient name for the Holy Spirit

Mirror

This old Soul doesn't look in the mirror anymore,
Because faces are not the heart,
And this heart wears many faces.
Look into my eyes:
The world is still spinning, and I am older than a million years.
Where will you be tomorrow?
Catapulted to the sun or rocketed past Andromeda?
Take me with you, Mahanta,*
I want to be known for impossible flights!

* the inner teacher

The Sleeper and the Race

Where is this leading?
I'm like a treasure that was stolen
And changed hands hundreds of times.
With you I'm already here,
Wherever I'm supposed to be,
Still searching a road that leads to my heart:
    A city that never sleeps,
    An earth that never settles,
    Wind always escaping the hollow,
    An eagle that never lands.

How do I find my way not looking for peace signs,
Moving swiftly and lightly, seeking searing and burning,
Making way for rainbow signs,
As the Traveler makes way for the traveler?

You are all that I have, every noise has abandoned me,
And the pebble now speaks secrets to me
And iron in the mountain is now leading to gold,
Where I lay sleeping and dreaming.

Where is this leading?

In my mine of dreams show me a dream that is real,
The one where I am all that I am,
Or the one where I'm becoming all that I am,
Sooner or later they are one and the same.

This is the dream I am dreaming –
Treasure changing hands hundreds of times,
In a race to find the treasure within,
The race of a lifetime, heavens within.

Circular

Your language has but one meaning –
A circle that moves around my heart
From one breath to the next,
Never ending, always beginning,
Divine nectar filling up my heart,
God's silver water on my lips.

Take Me, Mahanta*

Greater than a billion suns, deeper than seas that feed the galaxy,
More peaceful than the world's sleeping babies,
Holier than the mystery of all ages,
Wiser than teachings buried and resurrected,
More loving than hearts which have ever beaten,
More joyful than the most golden dreams:
You are the True Messenger, Giver of Life.

The star I wear around my neck,
This band of gold on my finger – I am wedded to Life:
      My legs move to keep up with it,
      My face lights up with the expectation of bliss,
      My chest fills with a chorus of songs,
      My lips part to drink of eternal life,
      My mind is the knower of all things silent.
You, Mahanta,
Are building my house of consciousness
In this instant and forever since.
You look upon its gold and silver aspect
As ratios of perfect consequence,
And the lines are all figures of the Alone and You,
Nothing more than secret barriers to Your door.
Let me in – all of me –
To the entrance of your kingdom,
To find that I'm already yours,
And You are everything I ever wanted.

* a matrix for the Light and Sound of God

WRITING RUMI

Ocean

Show me the silver places on your ocean floor,
I'm living there now, a miracle.
I have fire in the water to see by,
And signals in the deep to hear by.
Give me air if I need to surface,
For I'm navigating with my heart only.

Evolution

When I was an amoeba what was I looking for?
To survive –
Now I'm here, just wanting to survive.

As a rock what was I learning?
Contentment and being –
Now I'm here, wanting contentment and being.

When I was a hawk what did I seek?
Freedom through mobility and speed,
All of my own making.

When I was a spider what did I endeavor?
A world in which I was sovereign,
Then laid it to waste.

What's the difference now that I am human,
Frail, flexible, denied –
Was I not better off unconscious?

Now I have contentment in knowing:
    Survival is Soul in eternity,
    With freedom comes responsibility,
    True power is divine love –
And these have made all the difference.

Order, Yellow and Rivers

Have I always seen it this way?
Just a moment ago I was a villain years old in crime,
Though I'd been accosting no one but myself.
Now like a new coin I shine upward in the palm of God
Rolling into a brook to be wished on.

[I drove all the weary horses to drink.
They'd raced long enough in the countryside
And escaped to open sky,
Where eagles meet and fly unobstructed.]

Is it a new time
Or just the advancement of new things?
I could swear I've never seen this before –
Before my God was the new-God-in-me.

Is this what I've come so far for?
The unequivocal flame of being
So finely tuned, bright and yellow-white,
That I weep at its trembling beauty?

I drink and drink,
Like a greedy man who died in a river
And has a second chance.
I laugh and laugh,
Like a mad woman who discovered she was sane,
Even when she lost everything she loved.

This is a new order of things:
The fine pale yellow of Soul-in-sky,
The view of water-water-everywhere,
And all the rivers which are my ardor
For the one, shining thing I am.

It's peace that I've found
In those starlit loves of yesterday,
In the rainbows shimmering seven-in-one –
Now angels are sitting at my feet,
And I am worshipping the brilliant God of Life!

Famous for Zero Minutes, but Spiritually Active

From school house to a blue dome
From crackling earth to gold elixir
From snake pit to the marigold fields of summer
From the crimson plain of Avernus
To the white roads of Jupiter

What a journey I've been on
Galaxy shifts and gravity loops
Contortions of body and delinquencies of mind
Snapping limbs and hearts looping in terror

Heaven is never what I thought it would be
In a picture frame to be posted at the gate
Instead it frames the entirety of that not painted
Or sculpted or written or spoken or sung

From surprises to surety
From inadequate rations to a full house
From the gray cloud of collapse to a victory dance
From shame to the electric fame of the heart

What a place I'm going to
Where high wire acts and clowns have retired
Ferocious dogs are lulled into napping
And both light and dark are eclipsed by a Sun

Love is never what I thought it was
Something instinctual chanced upon by lovers
It's a creation of the highest order
A love of God architected as the calculus of Being

Magic

Trickster, trickster, cookies in a jar,
Master, master, coming from afar,
Rockets, rockets, shooting from my head,
Dancers, dancers, reeling in the dead.

Swoon, swoon, carry me aloft,
Swim, swim, guided by a falcon,
Coo, coo, singing in a woodland,
Ego, ego, put it in a box!

Desert, desert, eating up the fountains,
Brook, brook, climbing up a mountain,
Ash, ash, burning in the desert,
Wind, wind, sailing down a river.

God, God, can you hear me answer?
God, God, I'm living out my destiny,
God, God, I am full of pleasure,
God, God, what are all these symphonies?

Write, write, seek you out a fable,
Cry, cry, tears are but your fantasy,
Love, love, this is like my glimmer twin,
Bathe, bathe, the Ocean has the answer.

Bliss, bliss, see it in the eyes you have,
Knowing, knowing, give life all you ever had,
Kiss, kiss, give it to your next of kin,
Blow, blow, the wind will seed the field you're in!

Melody Frees the Warrior

With your Word I raze obstructions,
Dizzy with sign and symbol,
I approach the altar of divinity and reason.

You turn me on a fork of celestial melodies
Vibrating the length of life,
And I do what your Grace asks of me –
Sing, listen, and create now from the Word.

Circle me at infinite speeds with your wand of Being
Fending off the giant who disappears millions of selves,
Setting me free to love You,
So I can leave the battlefield.

Everything I Love

Sound, bread and wine,
Everything I love is in this cup,
One container in a sea of cups
That hold the secrets I must know.
Secrets only remain, they are forever my days,
As the ancient Light and Sound roll on.

Golden coins of Soul wash onto shores of my heart,
Yet I'm already rich and want to give them all away –
For if gain is God, then loss is only wanting God.
Hasten opening of this sea,
Hasten the emptying of this treasury!

Spiritual Exercise

I love your spiral flame,
The way you invite me into the center of the eye,
Into the middle of your hurricane.
Your gaze tightens the bowstring,
And golden arrows shoot straight into the heartland.

You are the Friend who brings lavender and roses
And lays my head upon your golden heart.
You are the invisible lover who loves me even when I am gone,
Who speaks ceaselessly of me, as I do You,
Though silent.

Translation

If I was to die what would I say:
    That I've never laughed so hard,
    That I've never hurt so deeply,
    That I've never loved so intently,
    That I've never regretted anything?

My life is a treasure house for holy dreams,
A rolling red carpet for kings and queens
    who populate it – gifts of God –
If only they could see.

I see you, I know you, I love you.
I will say it again and again,
I thank you.

To the blood line that birthed me I say:
Seek the Golden Heart that gave you breath.

To the love of my life I say:
Had I known you better I would have doubted less.

To the God in me and you I say:
Take me elsewhere that I may serve Thee better,
For my Home is anywhere I choose to love.

This is a translation any Soul will understand.

Alchemist

The forge of the alchemist
Grows cold and hot by degrees
Every which way combines and segues
Around the circle of spiritual science.

I cut the grass of the Arabs,
Luminati, lux and lumen –
Threshed and boiled the emerald blades
Till they sharpened the air about the sun.

As the Master protects the pupil of Soul
I pass through the ring-of-pass-not,
Cleansing the silver eye,
That quicksilver orb of Beauty.

Twenty-First Century Writer

I want to light upon your star
And beat a drum of love among the planets.
Heart open, I'll announce your coming to the world,
As if you had ever left.

We're making your presence known again
Announced by the wind, the bleating of oceanic storms,
And hail from ancient planets –
But declarations of love are the oldest documents.

With Your light and melody pulsing in my veins,
I gather my bodies around the diamond of renewal,
Writing again and again for the Living Word.

In the House of Love

If I can hold it in my hands without burning,
Receive it in my heart without fainting,
Illusions fly out of this red attic of desire.

Monkeys still hide in the silver linings of this house,
But your spiritual fire is cool, ethereal and blue.

If I bend my ear I hear an echo of exploding truth,
And all things are blessedly re-arranged.

Found

You found me under sedimentary rock
And five layers of river bed.
Now you rouse me,
And I dream of the ways you will teach me
So I can stand your beauty while awake.

How you seek me!
Like an adventurer in a new country
You claim an empire in your disciple,
A once and future King.

Identity

You pulled me from hearth and home
Carrying only the banner of Identity.
I know you –
I am Soul, and you are my life.

Love settles on me like dust after a long battle,
And the army of love now worships in a sweet grove.
Holy ones pour golden nectar in my mouth
And sweet water of wisdom in my eyes.
Wandering drunk through the forests of perception
I follow the perfume of a Great Oak,
Hundreds of blue birds flocking to its limbs.

Your Name

If you want to know any order in this world,
Sing your name and hear how it rhymes with God's.
Infinite harmonies roll off your tongue
As you move your entire body into Its ocean.
A conductor is sending you messages from his white baton,
And your old bones sing a maritime splendor.
The ship of your life embarked eons ago,
And the navigator was the Mahanta, the Living ECK Master.*
When you hear the sirens of futures past,
Look inside the living Soul for direction,
Rolling forever on the ocean of the HU.*

* a being whose only mission is to help a Soul return home to God; given
respect but never worship
* the voice of God

Questions

Questions are like snakes –
They coil around you and strike,
Poisoning by simply being.
To find an answer don't go seeking –
Like lifting a rock only to find slugs
Or beating a closed door with your head.
Be silent and all questions will come and go
Like a snake slithering away in the hot sun
Winding back to you illuminated, having shed its skin,
De-fanged by the Snake Charmer.

Miracle

A kernel is the entire field you till for me,
A tiny root is the orchard where you planted apples.
An invisible star is a blaze of enlightenment,
And each step I take is the journey fulfilled.
In every part of me am I whole in you,
From large to small and small to large,
From the invisible to the visible, and the visible to the invisible.
Soul is changing in your love,
Like oil miraculously mixing with water.

Answer Me

Answer me, O God,
Though I have no questions –
I am only Soul asking to serve.

Fill me with gifts,
And as I am full I will empty out,
Though I am not fit to wash Thy feet.

Like a molecule floating in an atom,
I have no clue about the breadth of its circumference
And lose myself on the circle, eclipsing Love's boundary.

You fill me with golden deeds
Dropped in the wide expanse of Soul,
Touching this one and that one.
O Joy, O God!
Let me *be*, I ask of Thee!

This Place

This place is like a sonnet, a free glass of water,
The trees are like sky, and the sky is like heraldry,
The moon is eternal and now I know why.
The miracle that draws me to you is simple:
There's no line to draw, no face to put on,
No decision to make, no lies to tell,
I walk around your love like a kaaba,
Circling and circling until I can't get out,
For everything in life is in me, in You!

Birthday

When God created you on the birth day of Soul,
Seas of laughter rose from the tide,
Delivering a form on the wave of life
To a thousand planets, a million names,
Lost and found,
A seed of sound planted on rare earth
To become an oak of God.
Shining seed of God who made thee,
The fruit of heaven that feeds thee,
On your birth day in a sea of miracles, we celebrate
The sound inside you, God's holy breath in form,
Ever into the Formless.

Let Me Be

Rivers of ice and ovens of fire,
Let me be the love I desire,
Temper me on the ground of being,
Then set me loose on the roaring Sea!

Beginning

Pearl – when it's taken from the shell,
Stone – when it becomes the temple,
Human – when s/he becomes the initiate,
Body – when it becomes knowledgeable,
Soul – when it begins the journey Home,
Love – when it opens the heart.
Spirit sweetens matter, beginning at the beginning,
In every age.

Beyond

Beyond love and friendship,
Beyond teacher and student,
Beyond priest and worshipper,
Beyond horse, eagle, rock or flower,
Beyond France, Africa and atomic collisions,
What we are to each other is always in the Music –
Beyond any pull of gravity, you will always accompany me
On the Mahanta's* golden road.

* the Light Giver

God Loves

From the outside of the bark to the inside of a tree,
God loves you.

The fish shedding water and trembling in the net,
God loves you.

A dog in the lap of an old man, pink tongue in his hand,
God loves you.

A nurse drawing blood at the bedside of youth,
God loves you.

A muse drawing poets to write at her table,
God loves you.

A moth that rises and enters the flame,
God loves you.

A heart beating wildly to follow Your voice,
God loves you.

Gaze

Gazing at You is like being a ship near shore,
Then departing to the farthest ocean.

Gazing at You is giving what I can,
Then receiving back all I am.

Gazing at You is listening to silence,
Then hearing the wisdom always spoken there.

Gazing at You is opening the door,
Then finding my heart always open.

Gazing at You is blessed rest,
While adventures of a lifetime play out before me.

Gazing at You is like winning in life,
Then life winning me over with happiness!

Spiritual Traveler

You are the path shining in the evening
Where spiritual treasure is waiting,
I approach and offer my heart completely.

Hour by hour, details reveal themselves
To be kisses on the robe of God,
Diamonds turning their faces up
In the holy stream where I cup my hands and drink.

When I travel through the mountain pass, please be with me.
I will cover all territory using your map
And rest only to wonder at these great heights.
Hearing my footfalls echo with yours, O Master,
Let us travel together, like eagles who live on air!

Speech

God's speech alights on tongues of the truly humble,
The same words and phrases of invisible speech
Which transmit from my heart to yours.
Friends in the garden and brothers in the Light,
We speak a language of hidden happiness –
Our hearts are catchers of golden rain,
And the wind produces there every kind of living thing.

Friendship

I thank God that God-lovers eat at my table –
Their words are the fruits of friendship,
And after discarding the skin, we taste only sweetness and fiber.

This House

Lightning is passing through this house,
Its windows framed in a white heat.
I'm laughing ten stories up where my head folds neatly into heart,
Having jolted the Sleeping Giant awake.

On the Way

Many miles is how far I've traveled to safety,
Arms pinioned against my back,
Hair standing straight up like a ramrod.
This is a best effort
To capture a white flag held at arm's length –
To kiss and be kissed,
To yearn and be yearned for.

Prayer cloths whipping about my knees
Are like the patter of wings on ice
Or drops of blood on a wishing stone.
But gratitude was never sacrificed,
And it's gratitude I will keep.

Out of ideas, what is there to wish for?
The silence has gone deep into a miner's stone,
I'm like Excalibur in this quarry where I roam,
Learning to live with folly and the flame –
Both light my way,
Both beast and burden carry me a mile,
The child and ant both smile at me directly.

I will give you all I have, for you are always with me,
Carry me a while as you sing me a song,
And I will travel lightly as we slay the miles.

Smitten

I wear You on my forehead like a sign
Burned into an all-seeing eye of Vision,
My sword of light humming in a rock of solitude,
Showers of stars erupting,
Mysteries escaping illuminated mountains.
I wear You like the world wears You –
Unaware of the gifts, yet secretly smitten.

Spiritual Space

What I feel is beyond heat and cold,
What I see is apart from the season.
You opened your cloak wide
And revealed worlds in your care,
A dance of veils and light
Stacked one upon the other.

In the deep breach of spiritual space
Your mission vibrates there leaving nothing untouched,
Like a daffodil shaking itself loose into roses,
Or a heart declaring its love forever.
Stars and moons, beginnings and endings,
All cling to your ancient, universal Word.

Circling

My love binds me to you, Mahanta,*
It is the altar on which I lay my desire to serve,
And the celestial drumming in my heart moves to the Source.
Your universes circle these golden atoms,
As I ride an arrow of Light and Sound back to you,
From you to me, and back again.

* the inner teacher who gives spiritual instruction

On Friends' Journey to India

Candles line a road to the devotees' house,
On the hearth next to the water ladle and cooking pot,
Fried fish tangy with a hint of poppy.
Caravans travel past bamboo and banana trees,
Surly pythons watching and never forgetting
    who did what to whom,
Our past lives in India are roped together like flowers.

Bent over oil lamps, running fingertips over Sanskrit mysteries,
I'm caught up in the flame of Govind, the wayfaring son,
    the holy mother and devoted daughter,
Studying under lime trees and worshipping
    under the banyan tree,
Along our steady pilgrimage to Delhi.

In a thousand years not much has changed but the names,
The devotees have come around again to hear the teacher,
As the Madhava Lion stands guard for golden scripture,
On the long royal road to meet Mahanta-Vishnu.

Awake

In the Master's world,
    everything is awake,
Nothing is asleep,
Not even the sleepers.

Galaxy

Put your galaxy on,
Brush the stars between your teeth,
Wipe the meteor clusters from your brow,
Paint your cheeks with noonday suns,
And comb your hair back with the wind of God –
It's time.

Show Me

I feel fierce in wanting to reach the realization of God,
Taut, like I'm strung to fit the bow of love
And shoot directly into the eye of God.
If war would be love, I feel like the member of a golden horde
Ready to lay waste to anything between me and IT,
Restless and desirous of only one thing.
I'm not afraid of death,
And if Life is the only means to obtain the prize
Then I will live till there is no more breath in me,
Getting what strength I need from the ECK.*
Show me how I may serve love in this world,
Something that takes my whole being all of the time,
A constancy of dedication,
A vibration that I vibrate to on the God bow,
So I know I am the golden arrow –
Show me, show me, how I am the ECK!

* Divine Spirit

Fly

What remains? The remains.
On the high road, I meet an eagle
And she is me.
Fly away, my dear,
My bold winged thing,
And know your place.

Alive

I'm alive with the infinite plan inside me:
It's colorless yet I see its color,
Shapeless as a vowel, but it is my breath,
Bodiless as incandescent stars,
And alive as sinuous flesh.

Gift

You've given me a gift, this present moment,
The vibrating ring that weds me to you
At the heart of everything.

I've placed it on my hand,
And I'm already gone.
Like spots vanishing from a leopard
Or rain clouds evaporating in the noon sun.

The present moment chases me down,
Always where I am.

Blue Diamonds

I looked in this box in the dark
And the lid was closed
But the light shone,
And inside blue diamonds.
A blue light in the dark
Shone out from the box,
I opened the lid
To history unrolling –
The coloring book of life,
And in it a pen of blue fire –
Blue diamonds.

Offering

A being in green offered me growth,
A being in red offered me greatness,
A being in yellow offered me beauty,
A being in blue offered me peace,
The God-man offered me everything,
And I went up.

True Direction

Over ominous rocks, boiling seas and shipwrecked shores,
Carry me on a wave of eternal Song to my destination:
The saving grace of SUGMAD.*
The Master says: *Sail on, sailor.*
I won't tarry or watch for signs,
I'll keep beat to the music of my heart only,
To a sunrise that beams beyond every starlit shore,
My home and heart reside there.
Sail on!

* another name for God

Arrow

My love is like an arrow I draw back
To pierce the veil of my own illusions.
Guide it to the mark, O Master
And be my guiding light,
So I may serve Thee better in all worlds
Of your Truth and my becoming.

What I Need

I've forgotten words, time, and my own name.
How could I have forgotten for so long?
You've encouraged me onto this ground of holiness,
So how could I ever stray from you, never being far off?
What you've laid on my doorstep is still invisible:
A rope to climb with, a telescope to see the sights,
But even these I do not need:
My eyes are stars,
My head is the earth,
My body gives birth to planets,
And my heart is the sun of this world.

Last Time

A golden light awaits at the end of a tunnel,
I've been here before,
This is the last time I will dream this.

No human is awake who has not tasted the adventure
    of Divine Love –
To walk in one direction and read from a single book,
To become One, with no other place else to go,
Seeing that Light for the first time – going at God's direction –
For the very first time.

Loved

I am the beloved,
You are my Beloved,
Anywhere I seek, you have loved me.
Always within reach,
You have no circumference,
Knowing no center,
So all around and within:
The love of the love of the love –
So great it exceeds the heart,
Into the greater expanse of Eternal Soul.

Love me, O Beloved,
You are my Paradise,
I live for you in this and every world.

Flame

I saw a tree on fire – a living flame –
But nothing was destroyed,
It only increased and gained.

I threw my trinkets in the fire,
Attachments around my neck,
They disappeared like molten lies
And passed away like breath.

The flame of God lives in my heart
Burning the trunk of material woes,
My heart is like its holy root
Whose branches burst through sky and cloud,
To God.

Your gaze has been the holy spark
Igniting love so many years ago –
Never to be extinguished again it lives in me,
And forever will be so!

Ransom

There was a price on my head,
But I gave it up,
There are no more tales to tell.
The God of life speaks through me,
I can't be bought or sold,
You can have everything I am,
No charge.

Love

Look at Love spinning above,
Beyond silver moon and sun
Shimmering around the Ancient One.

A miracle of mind and matter,
Ancient and new, formed and formless –
Me and you and time forgotten,
The great and small in love remembered.

In Its vastness is a repository of all names,
In Its depth a reservoir of all beauty,
In Its silence the power of all vows,
In Its power the love of all seekers,
An anvil upon which Golden Hearts are beating.

Beyond

Beyond the grasping fingers of illusion, Love –
Deep, kind and secure with a face of peace,
The warrior who flung the gauntlet into space
Has broken his sword and gone home.
Was the war won,
Was it ever waged?

As long as truth is, we are,
And the All graces us with a vision of peace long in coming,
Way beyond the telling of our tales.

Silver Circle

A circle of love is above and below me,
Has it always been?
The net of love that caught me,
Is the one that tamed me,
Is the one called Love.

Two skeins wind about me
Cut by the hand of God.
Two flowers intertwined
Are tied with a cord of wonder.

If I fall, I rise up to the next heaven,
A canopy of love fluted with weightlessness.
The world goes round,
And the Word goes round and round.

Swimming in a pool of wisdom
Your Body is a mirror.
If I catch You I may dream,
For the pool is circular,
And I may dream and drown again.

A circle of love is above me,
It has always been,
A circle of love is below me,
I have always been!

www.ingramcontent.com/pod-product-compliance
Lightning Source LLC
Chambersburg PA
CBHW031846090426
42741CB00005B/374